D1443580

THE TRANS-SIBERIAN RAILWAY

by Cornelia Veenendaal

Copyright © 1973 by Cornelia Veenendaal
All rights reserved
Library of Congress catalogue card number 73-86246
ISBN 0-914086-01-4
Printed in the United States of America
Second Printing September, 1974

Book design by Judith Fletcher
Cover drawing by Mary Austin

These poems were published originally: ESKIMOS in *Commonweal;*
SHADOWLESS in *Inscape* at the Baleen Press; THE MALLARD in
Michigan Quarterly Review; WALNUTS FROM ATTAR in *The
Masked Media* (University of Massachusetts—Boston); APSARAS ,
AT MIDDAY I SLEEP, MS. VAN WINKLE'S SHORTEST MONO-
LOGUE, READING ABOUT THE NORTH CAPE CRUISE TO
LENINGRAD IN THE OFFICE OF H. & R. BLOCK, ABC in
Hanging Loose.

ALICE JAMES BOOKS
Cambridge, Massachusetts

For Barbara

CONTENTS

I

11 Between Bridges
12 My Grandmother's Geraniums
13 How Many Gardens
14 A B C
15 Catherine
16 If They Fall They Become Eagles
17 Walnuts from Attar
18 Orpheus Visits an Old Woman
19 Listen
20 Asparas

II

23 The Mallard
24 The Primrose Path
26 Eskimos
27 On my Fourteenth Wedding Anniversary
        I Ride on Trains
29 Sometimes We Were
30 Patchouli
31 Rain
32 After Rain, Fortune, 2 Oct.
33 Wife's Story
34 Farewell

III

37 At Midday I Sleep
38 Under the Snow
39 Shadowless
40 Harrow
41 Compensation is at Work, Beginning
      with the Moon
42 "The Crucial Problem in Flying
      is Control of Equilibrium in the Air"
43 The Sun is Thorough in Gloucester
44 Now I Can Roar
45 This Calendar Year I See Who I am
46 Dream Journeys
48 A Summary

IV

51 Pictures from a Freshman Text
52 Saint Patrick's Day
53 Reading about the North Cape Cruise to
      Leningrad in the Office of H. & R. Block
54 Salvation Army Band, Wait for Me
55 O July
56 Rip Van Winkle's Dream
57 Ms. Van Winkle's Shortest Monologue
58 "Despite all his Careful Preparations, Nixon
      Is Facing Many Unknowns on his Visit to China"
60 Why Am I Looking Forward
62 Celebration

1

BETWEEN BRIDGES

The smooth path curves
in a sweep of grass
and blue corn flowers.

A wind from the river
ripples my sleeves.

       I can't bear it.

       I have become my father
       and my mother.

If I were still myself
I might be walking here
in high sunlight forever.

But the bridge grinds
its stones and I will strike

trolls from its cracks
when I get there.

MY GRANDMOTHER'S GERANIUMS

I used to play
around my grandmother's plants
depressed by ferns, hating begonias
but the quince tree on the lawn
I proudly acknowledged.

In the park why did we have
to drive to the rose gardens?
Or strain our necks to see
the peacock listlessly
shuffle his sparse fan?

I longed to go inside
the rank forbidden house
where monkeys lived their
clever, guiltless lives,
and the lion, waking, raised
his wasted voice against us.

HOW MANY GARDENS

How many gardens have been dug
near despair?
Better than plunge the blunt tools
in oneself, plunge
them in earth.

I can see my father
kneeling beside his long beds
of scarlet gladioli
with thunder building
in the marl overhead.

I know, thinking back
on those summers,
his work, so festively
responding, was powered
by his storms.

Rage pouring into his arms,
his hands, did not infect
the bulbs' cool reserves;
their soon to soar fibers
were not frayed by trembling
in a human touch.

Oedipus — what he touched
when he counted himself happy —
rotted to death.

A B C

One of the things
fourteen can do
is learn the deaf alphabet.
When everyone is shouting
around you, it's handy
to talk to yourself
with quick wingy letters.

From the window
I watched your taxi
driving off late.
All I could see
inside the dim car
was your hand
jabbing curses at the air.

CATHERINE

In a nursing home that seems
to be flying — past fields grown thick
as stories, past trees, high over
and west of town and harbor —
an old patient wanders with walker
out of her room, down the hall
and back, and cannot rest,
beside herself, feeling betrayed.
Other wrinkled bones that wake
and sleep in pain may never see
again the wings they are under,
but no one is so out of self as she,
who cannot wish to make the consuming
journey to the dining room,
where, glassed in like a starship,
the tables are ready with bright
goblets for a feast.

IF THEY FALL THEY BECOME EAGLES

Radishes celery lettuce
my hands work with a knife
under cold water. Suddenly

father and mother
as if they still lived
in their house, were still

of the same planet.
Be well! My care (for whom?)
tilts with speculation:

if they could have fallen,
they might have become eagles.

WALNUTS FROM ATTAR

small as nuts
my father used
to gather, satin
skinned, tasting deep

but today every
walnut I crack
has a fat white
worm, and two
gray moths
parade like duennas
through the jar

ORPHEUS VISITS AN OLD WOMAN

1

He walks lightly, gliding
looking always ahead. His eyes
are in the world with love.
Fearing but never resting,
he is alone with his songs.
He sings for the snow,
for the stalks that reach up
like dead nerves
through the white snow.

2

You are sitting still.
Your head does not turn
when I tell you I am well.
Your hand does not lift
when I give you my present.
Your hands shake,
but that is with agitation
that someone is asking them
to take hold again.

3

A misshapen heavy dog
with a sore leg
quivers in his sleep
on the floor.

LISTEN

On a winter afternoon
out near the dunes
thrown up by new foundations,
you may hear
something like words.

They seem to say,
"I was the woods,
pines, moss dark and
streaming with resin,
barkless grey shells of oak,
fiery green boughs
making a nest
for a pale trembling sun.

I was shaded ground
taking back every fallen thing:
leaf, feather, snowflake,
needle of light.

Bluejays went their
piercing ways,
grosbeaks played around
my magic and inviolable trees."

APSARAS

The angel arrives
      in a swirl of clouds
  and rising water.

Nothing spills from his
      bowl. In the center
  of his gale he smiles

where I am standing
      in a fall of sticks
  or jumping clear of

the chop of blades. He says
      "Of course we are here,
  just as you are there."

Once in ten years our
      children may catch the eye
  of an asparas

when they are fading
      through the falling snow
  or halting bandaged in

a hospital hall.
      Even across great
  distance his curving

energy sends itself
      in a smile that is
  humanly given

one to one.   *(Relief from the ceiling of a*
                   cave in China, 6th century)

2

THE MALLARD

To be a pilot of the inland waters and the air
he has become a form touchingly subtle
and wears a shirt of fat where
he is diamonded with seven sober colors.
Setting forth he turns his brilliant paddles,
or floats in icy ponds. In the heights
of his migration he rows over whole states.
In reedy shadows summer nights
he gives his plainspeech criticism,
flaps open irridescent plans.
The mallard is for happiness in marriage;
no breach in his body or in his habits
lets trauma drive its wedge.

THE PRIMROSE PATH

Some primroses have come to us
from as far away as the mountains of India.
Long before spring they may
break through a cover of dry oak leaves
like poems, or like
falling in love in winter.

Do you remember, said Mary Lamb
to Charles, when we used to buy
strawberries and tickets to the shilling gallery?
And the time you ran out
at ten o'clock to buy the folio
Beaumont & Fletcher? How poor we were!
Always wearing the same coats.
It was the best time, though.
— Because we were young, said Charles.

*

Bursting upon the lawn
where Delius sat like death in France,
Percy Grainger pushed the skeleton
in a wicker wheel chair as fast
as he could run. Then everyone
in that sinister retreat came to life
in a sudden gust of health!
They remembered how, years before
in Norway, Percy and a strongman
had carried Delius in a chair up the side of
a long snowy mountain
to the sun.

*

Now I could run
out through the frosty air
laughing myself free
of the yearlong winter briars.

At least

I've pasted pictures of the primroses
on the kitchen wall
where I can see them
making a path for me.

ESKIMOS

1

One is a carved madonna
who walks on stiff legs,
peers from gouges with consternation
at a sky so densely green
the snow beneath her feet
reflects it blinding.
On her back a little baby sleeps;
her hands are free to balance
and to hold a pawlike knife.
All concern is she, all mass,
and thus she tells of lastingness.

2

The other one who casts
his numinous spell
is the artist carving the madonna.
He sits beside the ice wall,
wearing a wool cap and heavy parka.
His hands, smooth as walrus,
are bringing forth the little object
out of stone. There is his profile,
absorbed in finding form.
His eyes crease with amused joy,
and thus he tells of lastingness.

ON MY FOURTEENTH WEDDING ANNIVERSARY
I RIDE ON TRAINS

1

The one-coach Penn Central is bound
for Albany, but it stops at Back Bay
to take on a few commuters.
The conductor gives us a hand
up the back steps and we file in
through the snack bar.
If ever it turns spring
and we have a hot afternoon,
I'll get a can of gingerale.

But today is still as drab
as an Army-Navy store and I
settle down among newspapers
beside the rank ivory wall
and heavy lidded window, under
the tossed coats and shopping bags
on the luggage rack and thank God
for the smooth old pacesetter.
Alongside the turnpike streaks by,
then come the trees and towers
and houses among trees, all
powdered with predicted snow.

Where's my book?

2

The great Pullman was whirling onward
with such dignity of motion ... the
plains of Texas pouring eastward.

"Ever been in a parlour-car before?"

"No," she answered; "I never was.
It's fine, ain't it?"

"Great! And after a while we'll
go forward to the diner and get
a big lay-out. Finest meal in the world.
Charge a dollar."

"O, do they?" cried the bride.
"Charge a dollar? Why that's too much —
for us — ain't it, Jack?"

"Not this trip," he answered bravely.
"We're going to go the whole thing."

He pointed out the dazzling fittings
and her eyes grew wide as she took in
the sea-green figured velvet,
shining brass, silver and glass,
the wood that gleamed as darkly
brilliant as a pool of oil.
The ceiling was frescoed
in olive and silver ... . *

---

* Stephen Crane, *The Bride Comes to*
  Yellow Sky

28

SOMETIMES WE WERE

A crowd of moonshot marigolds
with bees.
We were
crinkled pale gold
a march in green
out of thin soil.

I never disbelieved them
but I knew   though nothing
seemed to give out in the plants,
frost would come.

When it did, the marigolds
looked as if a rain of hot wax
had fallen on them.
They were darkly penetrated,
I pulled them out.

All day I saw them
lying like mourners
on the compost heap.

PATCHOULI

Lopakhin.   Yes, time flies.
Gaev.   What do you say?
Lopakhin.   Time, I say, flies.
Gaev.   What a smell of patchouli!
            Chekhov, *The Cherry Orchard*

                    *

wind
telephone poles   wind swirling
dust and   telephone bills

just holding on
                       trying to take
the next step
knowing   it could be
                       into deep water
with our loves
millstones   millstones

            tied to us.

            *

When you came in to wake me
I was sampling marinated
mint plant.   Other delectable
dishes were placed on a
glass table before me.

You had nougat!
and she, a trencher of cherries,
feasters and friends
by a pale blue wall.

We must have been vacationing
on the Trans-Siberian Railway.

RAIN

A great rain is falling
Brightening the autumn leaves
Splashing the grey light
With rinsed green, bathing
The window with sheets
Of cold rainwater, driving
Down, deepening the colors
Of tree trunks and houses,
Drowning the sounds of
Other doors, keeping us
In our separate places.
Dare to think:
When a great rain falls,
Everything, everything
Changes.

AFTER RAIN

The mailman is talking to a dog.
Now he's made his point,
hops into the truck
and drives away.   In every puddle
I see a fragment of my life.

FORTUNE

The old cock on the steeple
mostly looks broadside at me.
Now he turns so I can hardly see him.
What he does not calculate
is how cold I can be,
how free.

2 OCT.

Now when I see a folded letter
on the ground, forgetting myself,
I almost take it up to read.
(It may contain a sentence or two
I need to know) so desperate is
my struggle.

WIFE'S STORY

Bluets
        one here
one there
    growing in rubble
along the railroad track
like songs
        heard miles back

Over and over
I have looked at that cloudy slope
and at those riders
in fur hats and belted sheepskin coats
their faces turned away.
I have never seen what is in their eyes,
but I can believe
they are men crossing out of this life
leaving sadness behind.*

Something in me is joining them
some coldness perhaps
or some outgrowth of spirit.
For what has sadness been to me
(such years of it)
or to anyone
about whom I have been sad?

I will ride up the steep mountain path
into clouds, to the pass.
I will go over
into new country.

* from W. S. Merwin's *Horses*

FAREWELL

Mushrooms exhale the woods
reminding me of sheets of violet paper
with spore designs, brought to school,
and of a grassy spot before I went
to school, where a bird was buried.

Chantarelles reminded Ray
of being on bivouac in Neimegen.
Champignons reminded us
of Ser Dolmens, at the edge of Flanders,
who sent his children out to pick them
around the hooves of cows.

The young boy, Barnus,
was reminded by a lawn full of toadstools
in the Bronx, of safe mushrooms
he used to find in woods
at home, in Indonesia.

3

AT MIDDAY I SLEEP

Blissful as bees
In the perfection
Of their work.

Do I look through honey?
Or is it the sun
Prising my eyelids?

Open!
You're playing tennis,
Your partner is skilled.

Sealed off by membrane
(All my years)
Yet how I played.

UNDER THE SNOW

I've been in slumber curled
Like a creature in its lair
Dreaming of wandering
On some quest of the dark world.

Along arboreal malls
I find my way alone
And up strange stairs
To a cavernous feasting hall.

Around the empty board
Are gathered my old friends;
My escort (merely a head)
Chooses one for his bride.

And suddenly manifest
He stands a man made whole;
I marvel at his diplomacy
That clears an impasse of soul.

All leave, then I am awake,
Bathed, dressed in clean clothes;
I stand in the church, a dance
Begins in my stolid bones.

SHADOWLESS

There are many people in our civilized society who have lost their shadow altogether.

C. G. Jung

Like a child who has forgotten a scarf
I left my shadow in the skaters' house;
It is waiting near the fire for me,
Bereft in the luminous city.

Under fluorescence what am I
But a poor blanched thing, knowable
As a manual of shorthand; skin exploding,
A wire voice that must be mine speaking

Trivia.   All the while the jade plant,
The violets grow to heroes in the cold
Lightfall, under ceilings purple and white
That so belittle me.   Some night

The skyscraper, mammoth honeycomb,
Its cells packed solid with light, may
For a moment go dark; and I shall dance
Candled and grotesque as Fritellino.

If not this, then I must go back
To the mountains, to the skaters' house,
To stand before gold fire blazing on stone,
To mend my life with my waiting shadow.

HARROW

There was a kind of harrow
That took one back to the Stone Age.
It was made of boards joined together
About the size of a kitchen table.
In the boards hundreds of holes
Were morticed and into each hole
Was jammed a piece of flint
Chipped into shape exactly
As men used to chip them
*Ten thousand years ago.**

George Orwell found this horror
In a Catalonian hut.
What was it?

This harrow, dragging slow,
Is what wakes me
Now, as long ago,
To what I have to do.

*Homage to Catalonia

COMPENSATION IS AT WORK,
BEGINNING WITH THE MOON

The tide is turning
Slowly
Beginning its ingress
Over sand, torn plants, cracked
Shells. We were scared
It would never turn,
But at last
It is turning.

A wind swarms through the fir trees
Bowing them before the theater.
The dancers have already arrived
And now the audience is gathering,
All under the direction
Of the resilient moon.

They dance in white flounced dresses,
Toothed, fluttering pennants high step by,
A live blue stream shimmies
Straight across the stage.
They are dancing
In the water.

"The Crucial Problem in Flying is Control
of Equilibrium in the Air"
Wilbur Wright

The fine new moon has come
to set me free. Its linen
crescent like a laser
picks at my tangle of
knots and floats them out.

I mount the blue wind
trawling for omens
that may take me
as hymns upon the voice
into the altitude of praise.

THE SUN IS THOROUGH IN GLOUCESTER

Light as air on portraits and willow china,
making it clear how the minister's desk
transcends the card table.

In the captain's bedroom, a mirror
is waiting for the captain's question
should he dare ask it.

The maid's sleigh bed is cool in the
browsing sunlight. The nursery
collects spangles off the sea.

It is like being drawn up in a seine of light
after a dark engagement of the deep.

NOW I CAN ROAR

My father my mother struggled
in a cruel undertow.
I dangled from a parachute blue
as the Duc du Berry's skies.
I knew the farmer and his ground
but from an angle, looking down.

In air my simple rooms
all intersect like courtesy—
night brings me fears out of
the hemlock air: nobody cares.

This is how it has always been with me
I don't complain.
But when I found the moon—
my moon in Leo when I was born—
suddenly I could stop just gliding
up and down. I could sit on my haunches
and feel for all the world
like the king of the beasts.

THIS CALENDAR YEAR I SEE
WHO I AM

Rama is young
his eyes are closed
he smiles
the lotus turns upside down
for him to dance on.

I am an elephant head
turned away,
my trunk half blown off
enduring. I hear him
snapping his fingers.

Sometimes his throat
itches from eating melon.
It is slow, it is hard
thinking him into words.

DREAM JOURNEYS

for Mary Curran

1

I'm going up the Hudson on an overnight
trip to my destination. On the tiny round
deck of my boat I'm sitting on a high stool.
I keep my eyes closed. If I look down
at the dark blue water all around me,
I'll get dizzy and fall off.
But I do open my eyes, and I'm in a ship's
cabin with two children, a boy and a girl.
I talk to the boy, promising that we will
play games on deck to pass time.
When I go out on the deck, I find a crowd,
whole families camping under canopies,
heating up casseroles over campfires.
A feast!

2

In a carnival seat I'm rushing upward
past ladder rungs at a breathless speed,
holding my brother, a child, in front
of me. He has a long sheet of paper
on which he has written a poem. He is
terrified. I say, "Don't worry, I'm
holding you tight," but the fact is, I'm
having a hard time keeping my hold on him.
I realize he is vomiting on the poem.
Later, on the subway to Cambridge, a young
red-haired woman passes me, saying,
"I'll show you where to sit because we
have to get off quickly at the next stop."
She disappears up a serpentine stairway
and I follow. In the large waiting room
above, she is nowhere.

3

All around me are snow covered peaks
and long snowy slopes. I have climbed
to this place the day before; now my old
friend joining me, I am getting ready
to climb to the summit. The day before
I wore strips of metal on my shins, which
reflected the sun brightly. I consult
with my partner and decide that I should
not wear them now, going higher, because
they may cátch too much sun.

4

This Russian city has gothic buildings
around a wide square. I am a tourist.
Betsy lives here. She invites me to her
apartment, shows me through a window
bodies of dead water buffalo lying on
the ground. She says the city does not
provide for taking them away and it's
unhealthy to leave them there.

5

Barbara and I are walking home
along a dark street of unfinished houses;
I say, "We've come this way once before,
it's not impossible. When we get to the end
we'll take a taxi home." Descending an
enclosed stair out of the long street,
I find in the debris of dead snow
two pairs of eyeglasses. One is too wide;
the other fits, but is pince-nez, entirely
metal, with one small lens, one large.
I put them on, they stick, but it's only
for fun. I mean to keep on seeing
with my own eyes.

A SUMMARY

I am supposed to bring sweetness
out of the carcase of a lion.
Down under the ribs, in thick shadows
I absently rummage.
In the upper branches of a huge
tulip tree a crow has landed.

The crow is thinking of his brother-in-law.
I am thinking of my uncle —

> perfectly tailored,
> his voice ravishingly cool,
> a master of intimacy
> that has no danger.

> Always on time.
> His sister, in a silk print dress,
> what did she not tell him?
> He pretended not to see
> the crow looking down.

Nor did he ever realize
that I was hunting for honey
in the hip sockets of the lion.

4

PICTURES FROM A FRESHMAN TEXT

two men are at work
on the growing arc
of a bridge   out over
the water of a bay
they wear long wrenches
like swords   sitting
on a girder   one man
tightens a bolt
the other standing
is looking for a match

in mild surf
two heavy women stand together
smiling   holding up dark dresses
to their knees
the sea air carrying sounds
the cold ocean washing their ankles
pleases them in an unfamiliar way

SAINT PATRICK'S DAY

Streetcars from Watertown
are wiping their windshields.

Louisa in a storm coat walks the dog.

My folded umbrella, when I swing it,
knocks against something behind me,
but there is nothing behind me.

How wet the buildings are!

Statues of the young gods
have been replaced
by poems painted on silk.

In stores cashiers
are wearing green carnations.

What! am I supposed to get up
at 9 o'clock just to go
to South Boston?

I tell you these things
because they are under the sun,
and because they are blurred
by gusts of rain
as we go toward the equal night.

READING ABOUT THE NORTH CAPE CRUISE TO LENINGRAD IN THE OFFICE OF H. & R. BLOCK

In a room like an old carton,
an envelope of stubs on my lap,
I half hear the discreet tax workers
telling poor people what they can't
deduct, can't claim as dependents,
then the adding machine, and the
parting, decorous as princes;
and half read that in the Hermitage
there is a golden clock as large
as a compact car, that on the hour
a golden peacock spreads his tail,
golden blossoms open, and wild life stirs.

SALVATION ARMY BAND, WAIT FOR ME

After the city councilmen shake hands
and march again, veterans in vehicles
roll by, a Red Cross unit, the high
school band, maroon among pink and blue
drum corps that blast and bang
and the smallest are carrying plastic guns—

comes the Salvation Army band
widely spaced on the street
playing a simple tune.
The drum goes on alone
sure of the beat and ample
in sober black and swinging
beautiful bearded young men.

O JULY

Occupying one space
By the brick wall
Of the bank, dust
And shreds, she is
The shade of an ancient
Hanging in still air
In Chester Cathedral.

Scratching,
In rolled orange
Stockings (not a pair)
And overshoes,
She moves some-
Where. She's going
To cross the street

On the arm
Of a fair boy.
Clean and bright--
What can he do
But turn his eyes away?
I hear her cooing
At his side.

RIP VAN WINKLE'S DREAM

He was used to getting news
When it was history, and so he heard
About the war after his friends had died
In it, or lived through it and gone
To Congress. He could not have dreamed
Of soldiers' white ruffed shirts
Turning to rags, in winter broken shoes
And empty kettles; plans and strategies,
Words more passionate than sun and rain.

If he dreamed, it must have been
Of feet marching to Albany, and slowly
Coming back, of hands foraging for berries
And firewood--he must have felt these shocks
Along the hill as a root feels them,
Or a groundhog, every pore asleep.

He came to the dark wood,
Slept, and then was welcomed home,
An amiable relic of the old yellow brick
Village, survivor of the fiery furnace
Of the virago.
                        All he wanted he was given
At last, a cosy life, a little fantasy.

MS. VAN WINKLE'S SHORTEST MONOLOGUE

I was only gossip. Mr. Knickerbocker
Didn't dare to bring me on his scene.
That would have mixed up his argument
All right!   He kept me out of sight
Like a mad cousin. I was the shrew,
The petticoat government. I was the loud
Voice that made the dog's tail droop.
Even my Judith, after she grew up
And married, could only say her mother
"Broke a blood vessel in a fit of passion
At a New England peddler."
I was behind the scenes, don't worry.
—If you ask me, we were all crazy.
But Rip was a thorn in my side
The size of a big wooden dagger, and that's
How come the village called me termagant.
Eh, eh, if I took time to think about it,
It was a lonely life. I was human, too.

A true wild horse still exists in Mongolia.

The northern complex included bear veneration
and fox myths, a matriarchal society.

The Yüeh culture was maritime and fluvial,
using long-boats, warships, and communal houses;
it had dragon myths, serpent worship,
and veneration of sacred mountains.
Records were kept on knotted cords.

Growing unrest among the people and the
technological revolution caused by the
coming of iron led to a demand, on the
part of the feudal lords, for advisors.
The Academy of the Gate of Chi, most
famous of the schools of philosophers,
was founded about the same time
as Plato's Academy.

Constantly the chamberlain quoted the Odes
and Annals to the Emperor, who ended by
becoming exasperated. "I conquered
the empire on horseback," he cried,
"what good is the Annals and the Odes?"
Lu Chia answered, "That is true, but
it is not on horseback that you will
be able to govern it."

Only the Taoists were irrepressible;
the Legalists had been liquidated.

The culture had driven deep roots
into the vast population of peasant farmers,
whose standards were Confucian or Taoist.
(They had not kept slaves.)

While the West worked with stars,
balls, levers, inclined planes and
chemical substances, China worked
with books, words, and documentary evidence.

   * * *

A tiny figure is getting out of a plane,
putting his foot down on vast unknown
ground, breathing in unknowing.
He thrusts out his hand, confident
that his preparations, briefcase
expertise, will pay off.

Joseph Needham, *Science and Civilization in China*, vol. 1.

WHY AM I LOOKING FORWARD

to waking up to snow?
to a few moments of exhilaration
in a winter of stony endurance?
Geese on the riverbank are eating seeds.
Last summer, sitting here in the sun,
I read the letters of Teilhard de Chardin.

> "Peking, Mar. 24, 1927
> A week ago I found, in the bottom of an old
> crate in the Licent Museum, a human incisor,
> very fossilized, taken by my colleague
> with some gazelle's teeth from the Paleolithic
> strata of Ordos. ... It is the first fragment
> of man in China."

The downsweeping branches are shining
with their loss. Sunsets burn them
and their structure remains.
When we have cold rain, I imagine
we are in Asia.

> "Tientsin, Apr. 20, 1927
> The whole country is undermined...and the
> English forces will not prevent the birth
> of a new China which is taking place. ...
> One may well wonder what is going to emerge
> from this difficult labor: an abortion
> or a real man."

The snow, when it comes, is mixed
with sleet. It freezes underfoot.
Blown beards of ice on rocks by the turnpike,
bare branches, fir trees, red and orange
berries are mesmerized.

"Tientsin, Apr. 30, 1927
We must create, by living it, an atmosphere
of new hopes, ambitions, and sympathies.
'Spirit' is a much greater destroyer than
violence, and it builds with the same
gesture with which it tears down."

CELEBRATION

Never buy a pineapple lightly;
    Only when everything
Seems to hang in the balance
    And you read there your belief
In the soul's struggle
    Or in life's need to swing back
At least halfway from reversals,
    Should you dare to celebrate
The year's shortest day
    Or the year's longest day.

Then carry the pineapple in
    Like a new king, establish
    Him among oranges and lemons
    Serene and absolute, from his
Hastate green crown (the cats adore
    With canine teeth)
To the underwater eyed rind clasped
    Tight over his radiant pale body
Growing sweet, growing bright,
    "His aspect and his heart."*

*A Song to David, Christopher Smart